FROM ROCKS TO ROCKETS

Arms and Armies throughout the Ages

William Gilkerson

First published in 1963.
This edition published in Great Britain in 2008 by Osprey Publishing, Midland House,
West Way, Botley, Oxford OX2 0PH, United Kingdom.
443 Park Avenue South, New York, NY 10016, USA.
Email: info@ospreypublishing.com

Previously published as *Gilkerson on War: From Rocks to Rockets*

A CIP catalog record for this book is available from the British Library

ISBN-13: 978 1 84603 423 7

William Gilkerson has asserted his right under the Copyright, Designs and Patents Act, 1988, to be
identified as the author and illustrator of this book.

Typeset in Square721 BT
Originated by PPS Grasmere Ltd., Leeds, UK
Printed in China through Worldprint Ltd.

08 09 10 11   10 9 8 7 6 5 4 3 2 1

For a catalog of all books published by Osprey please contact:

NORTH AMERICA
Osprey Direct c/o Random House Distribution Center
400 Hahn Road, Westminster, MD 21157, USA
E-mail: info@ospreydirect.com

ALL OTHER REGIONS
Osprey Direct UK, P.O. Box 140, Wellingborough, Northants, NN8 2FA, UK
E-mail: info@ospreydirect.co.uk

www.ospreypublishing.com

Osprey Publishing is supporting the Woodland Trust, the UK's leading woodland conservation charity,
by funding the dedication of trees.

To my warrior daughters Stephanie and Anna

IN THE BEGINNING...

Warfare lacked organization.
Methods were primitive.
There were no rules...
No uniforms... There was
only the gradual development
of weapons...

And CHAOS.

There are few records of
this era.

But significant strides were made, and eventually there were

ARMIES...

which, as the population expanded,
grew in size.

This increase in numbers made certain new concepts necessary.
There came...

the tactician...

the quartermaster...

and eventually, of course,

OFFICERS.

Soon there was CIVILIZATION
and the armies had uniforms,
and standardized weapons,
and discipline.

Warfare became more dramatic.
The people liked the color and the ceremony.
Man recognized the value of mobility...

...and he took to the water. He experimented with warships,

but early navigational techniques were crude.

Catapults were the first artillery.
They were used to throw
heavy stones and rocks,
but the GREEKS
used them to propel
great
balls
of
fire.

Among the early Greeks were the Spartans,
a people who were so much ahead of their time
        that they founded their whole culture on
        war.

The **ROMANS** came,
and they fought everyone.
During slack periods, they fought themselves.
They had heavy and light infantry.
They also had an elite guard
whose chief function was to protect
the Emperor and, at times,
to lead palace
revolts.

The Romans improved old war
machines considerably and invented
new ones of their own.

They made towers to carry their soldiers over walls.

They were taught the value of war
elephants by the Carthaginians.
Elephants were very formidable
and increased the mobility of the
Romans. Their armies moved swiftly
from place to place.

13

They had a navy.

They were so enthusiastic about fighting
that they made a sport of it (much as we do
now) and built arenas in which to stage
fights so that everyone could watch.

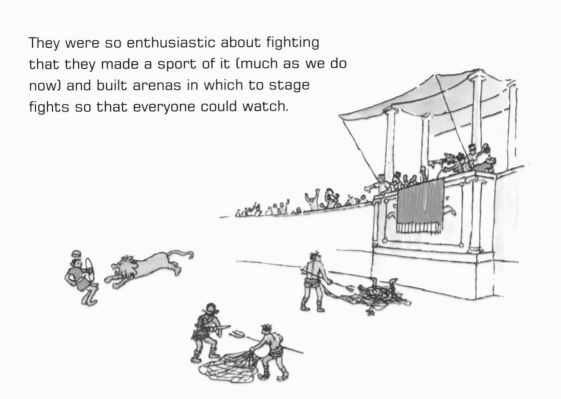

Their power declined
and Rome was beaten fairly conclusively
(two or three times) by the Goths
and by a numerous people from the East
called Huns

After the Romans came a period known as the

DARK AGES.

During this era almost no one was safe from anyone, and there was a good deal of disorganization.

It was the age of the Vikings,
who were from the far north.
They built efficient ships in which to
get at the people who lived in the south.
They were very fierce.

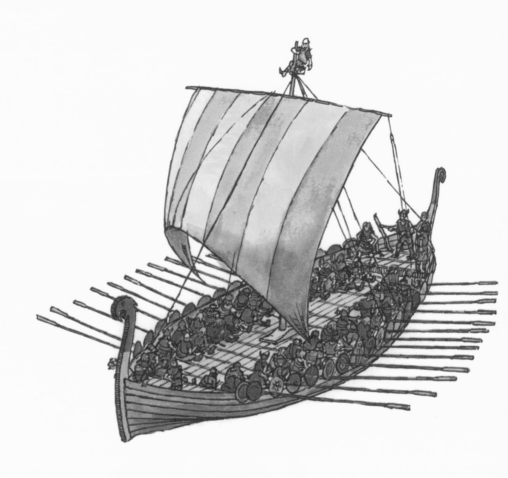

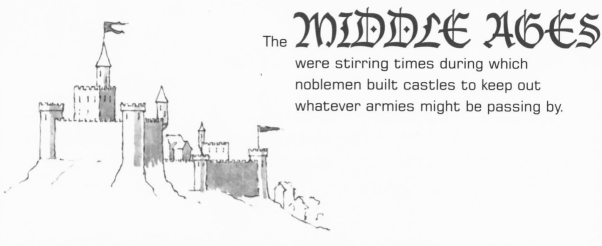

The # MIDDLE AGES
were stirring times during which
noblemen built castles to keep out
whatever armies might be passing by.

These castles had thick, high walls and heavy doors.

They were difficult to break into...

so bigger and better
war machines
were developed.

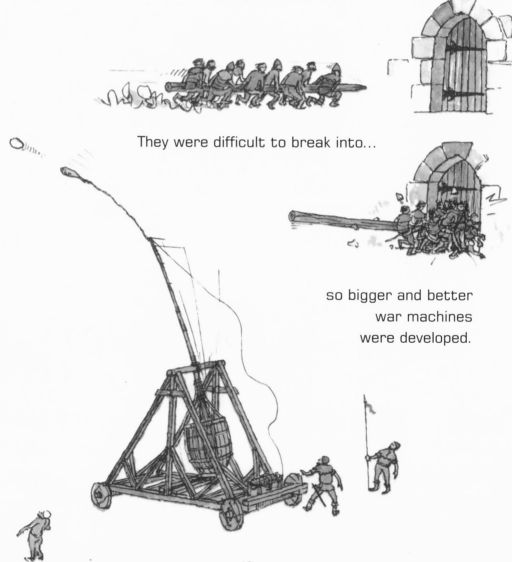

These were times of good kings

and evil kings.

They were times of merry outlaws who dwelt in the forests,
slaying the King's deer,

and robbing the rich of their money and their expensive garb.

They were times of great
quests, and dragons,
and fair ladies.

Eventually there came

GUNPOWDER

which was first thought to have
come from the Devil,

but which we later learned
was invented by
men.
It was used in huge cannons to shoot
big, round rocks.

By the time of the **Renaissance**, gunpowder was in wide use.
Many new weapons were invented during this period.
Some of these were useful…

...others were merely interesting...

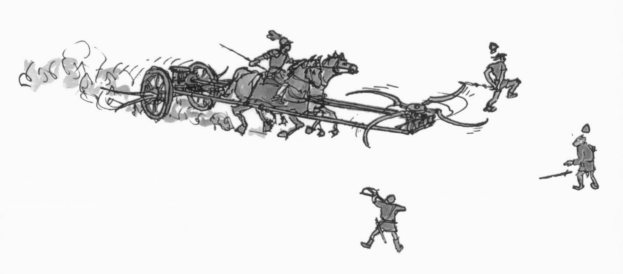

...and some were failures.

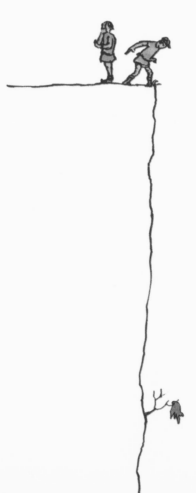

During the later part of this period Columbus discovered another huge area in which to fight. The Indians who lived there had, of course, already been fighting for some time, so everybody fought each other. The Indians lost.

As warfare advanced, foot soldiers were armed
with guns which they could carry with them.

Or they carried axes and hooks on long
poles to use against horsemen (who still
sometimes went around in armor).

Gentlemen fought politely with swords in
contests which their friends could watch.

Ships became bigger and more efficient.

Men learned to make more powerful guns. All foot soldiers were armed with them, and bayonets were used.

In America the rifle came into wide use. Successfully.

At this time, the Americans made a **REVOLUTION**.

And won.

Noting this success,
the French
made a revolution
also.

They also won, and their armies were (for a time) very powerful.

By the middle of the 19th century, there came a rapid advance in **INDUSTRY**. There were many new inventions which made dazzling improvements in warfare possible. Things got bigger.

Rapid TRANSPORTATION
resulted from the invention of the steam
engine, and armies were carried around
swiftly by rail.

There came balloons.

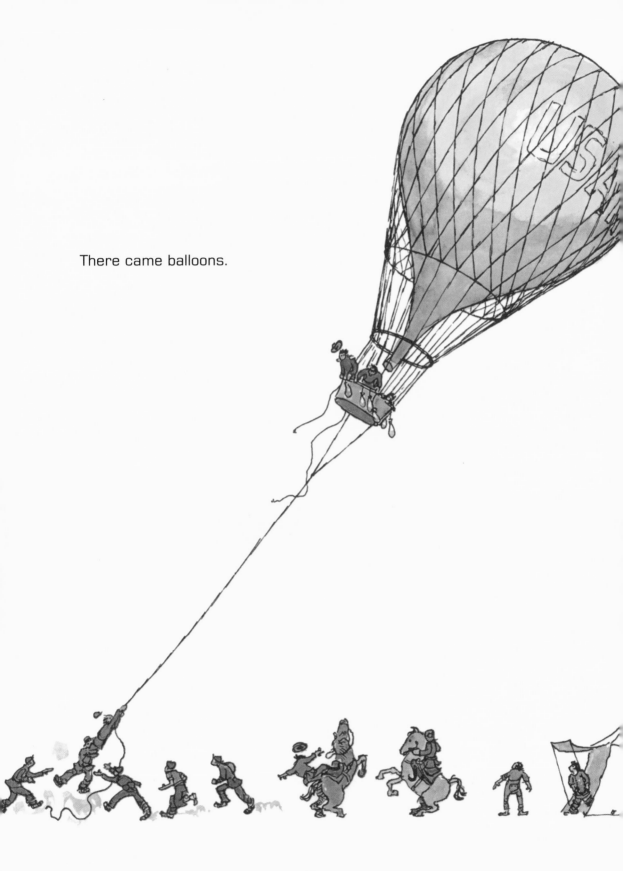

Everything
became
more
mobile.

Ships no longer needed sails.

All these new weapons enabled
the peoples who owned them to
take other, less fortunate peoples
under their protection.

The gasoline engine
opened even greater horizons,
and repeating guns were developed,

and finer cannons,
and gas.

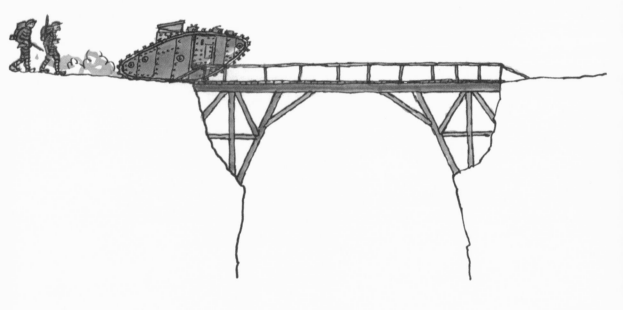

And heavily armored vehicles.

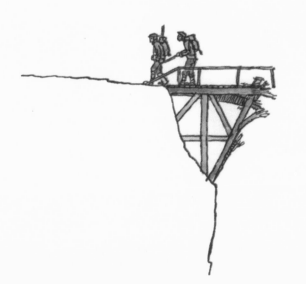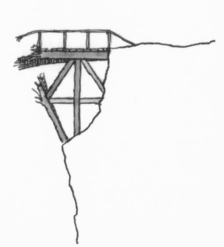

Man took to the AIR.

Everything
became
more
efficient.

Invention followed invention.

THE MODERN ARMY

has arrived at a high degree of organization.
It has many branches and departments.
Many of its people never see guns.
They organize and look after things.
There are...

supply men

and typists

and clerks

and medics

and their helpers

and cooks

and their helpers

and couriers

and generals
and secretaries

and public relations
men

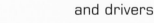

and drivers

and drill
sergeants

and instructors

and counterintelligence
men

and electronics
men

and police

And there is still...

THE INFANTRYMAN

The infantryman has newer weapons.

Improved vehicles allow ever-increasing mobility.

The army of today moves with lightning speed.

Armies
attack
by
air

...and by sea.

The seas are swept by larger ships than ever.

Aircraft of all descriptions have been used with excellent results,

but they have been largely replaced by un-piloted craft which can be controlled from the ground. These have become larger...

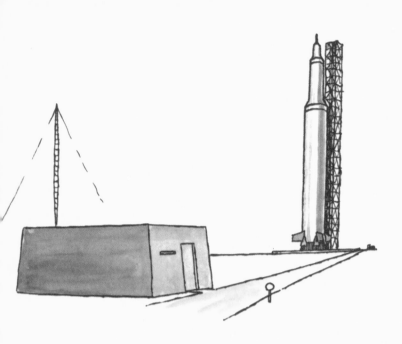

...and larger.

AT LAST...

warfare has organization.

Methods are no longer primitive.

There are rules...

and uniforms... and there is still

the gradual development
of weapons...

...and **CHAOS**